T0198867

THE COW

A Mother's Instinct Kicks In

Allyson Moore

Order this book online at www.trafford.com
or email orders@trafford.com

Most Trafford titles are also available at major online book retailers.

Printed in the United States of America.

ISBN: 978-1-4669-4981-2 (sc)
ISBN: 978-1-4669-4982-9 (e)

Trafford rev. 08/03/2012

 www.trafford.com

North America & international
toll-free: 1 888 232 4444 (USA & Canada)
phone: 250 383 6864 ♦ fax: 812 355 4082

Disclaimer

I would like to apologize to anyone who might be offended at the association that I have created between cows and my mother. Although the facts of these poems are true, I intend no maliciousness towards cows. Ultimately these poems serve to prove the supremacy of cows over my mother.

DEDICATION

To my dearest daughters. I have loved you since the moment that I knew that you existed.

CONTENTS

The Cow Question 1

Abandoned 3

Hallway Abandonment 4

Running Amuck 5

Anger 6

Annihilation 7

Piano Altar 8

Aunts and Uncles 10

Cover Exposure 11

My Bed 12

Communion 14

Angry to Death 15

Bow on Your Knees 16

Gender Denial 17

Wedding Suicide 18

Captivity 19

Will I Ever Be Rid of You? 20

Refuge? 21

Confession 22

No Intercept 23

Couches..24

The Crime...25

Culpable...26

Invisible..27

Fantasy Design.......................................28

Diabolic Mind..29

Trashed...30

No One Hears..31

Drunken Stupor.....................................32

Endure..33

To Live or to Experience..........................34

Façade..35

Spanking...36

Parent...38

Justice God..40

Guilty...42

Almost Homicide....................................43

Hatred..44

Androgyny...45

Living...46

Heart..47

Ulcers...48

Help Me..49

The Host...50

I the Man..51

Escape..52

Immolate 53

Never Could 54

Incest 55

Independent Birth 57

You 58

Age Inflicted 59

Murder Undetected 60

Truth Revealed 62

Jealous 64

Killing Set in Motion 65

It's My Life 66

Lost Opportunity 67

Accursed 68

Loving Myself 69

Madison 70

All Evidence to the Contrary 72

My Sister 73

Sacrificial Victim 74

Menses 75

Mother Mary 78

Blow 79

Murderer 81

Nietzsche and Kierkegaard 83

No One Wants the Responsibility 84

Penalty Box 85

Princess 86

Self Centered Drinking 87

Pleading the Fifth 89

No One Escapes.. 90

My Mind Abandoned Me.. 91

Professional Mother 93

Becoming Real 94

Sudden Recognition... 95

Repulsed.. 96

Lack of Communication 97

Fingered.. 98

Scars... 99

Sham 100

Alert to Attack 101

Sister 102

Reptilian 104

Standing Up.. 105

Weeping Mary 106

Paranoia 108

Surrogate Mom.. 110

Do Not Talk with Them... 111

The Beating 112

Nothing More to Expect... 114

The Remains.. 115

Signs of Trouble... 116

Vatican Deception... 117

The Whore of Halloween 118

To All the Addison's 120

Toddler Rape 121

Transparency 122

Naïve Twit 123

The Tyrant 124

Memories 125

Violation 126

Inward/Outward 127

Woods 128

Choice 129

Allyson's Requiem 130

The Cow 131

Locking the Gate 133

THE COW QUESTION

I first asked her when I was 12
"Did you want me?"
She looked me straight in the eye and said
"No"
"But when I saw you a mother's instinct kicked in"
I quietly said to her that cows do that
Turned and walked away

I was devastated hearing the truth
That was so obvious from her actions

At 18 I asked her the same question
"Did you want me?"
"No, I did not"
"But when I saw you a mother's instinct kicked in"
This time I said it a little bit more loudly
"Cows do that"
Turned and walked away

I was shocked that she had repeated the same answer
That she had given so many years prior

Somehow I had hoped
That I had misheard her
Misunderstood what she had said
Given her time to think
About her response
Then to change it
Or to lie to me

Twenty years later I asked her the same question
In the parking lot following Aunt Mary's funeral
"Did you want me?"
No, I did not
But when I saw you a mother's instinct kicked in
This time I screamed at her
"Cows do that"

Abandoned

Abandoned at birth
I have spent my entire life
Grieving
At the loss of not having a mother

Born
She screamed
That she did not want me
To come out

Abandoned in childhood
I spent those years alone
Without nurturing
Not sustained by a mothers love

Grown
I ran out of there
Seeking to find a mother figure
Who would unconditionally give her love to me

Allyson Moore

HALLWAY ABANDONMENT

Recovered from the rigors of childbirth
She eased herself out of bed
Heading down to the nursery
To seemingly cradle her newborn daughter in her
    arms

Ostensibly a tender moment
Until the staff and other patients
Realized that she was trying to give away
Her baby to anyone who would take her

The family doctor
Married and childless himself
Approached my father
Offering to adopt my baby sister

Despite my father's horror
He should have accepted it
Neither of them was fit to be parents
At least one of us would have been saved

Running Amuck

It would be better
If one knew how to give of themselves
Before they committed
To spitting a human out
From between their legs

A new life requires care
The ability to engage
In a creational process
Not in deviant behavior
From a drunken schizophrenic

It is a strange world
Into which we are born
Where the insane are allowed
To run amuck
Destroying their young

ANGER

Occasionally
There will be a day
When the anger chokes me
Slowly cutting off my ability
To breathe
Or to see the world
As a loving place for a while

It is during those times
That I head to the woods
Where the sounds outside my head
Mute the ones
Inside it
Where I can be one with the beauty
That is laid out before me

I need those reminders
That all is not bad with the world
That it's inhabitants
Are not reflective
Of its original source
That these justified moments
Will pass

ANNIHILATION

You struck at anything
Or anyone
That I loved

You sought to keep me
For yourself
Though hating me

Hurting those that I cared about
I kept my love hidden
Hoping that you would not destroy them

In obliterating them
You annihilated me
You are a beast

Allyson Moore

PIANO ALTAR

You desecrated the altar
Upon which the notes
Of my soul
Played themselves

The beautiful black Baby Grand
Sat silhouetted against
The backdrop of virginal white curtains
Overlooking a lush Garden of Eden

I sat before the keys mesmerized
In awe of the emotions
Dancing before me
Filling my spirit with glee

As a lover would touch the beloved
I gently stroked you
Took my time knowing you
Joining my body to yours

The Cow

Rarely have I known such bliss
Time suspended
We were one
Traveling in other realms

I never scaled that altar again
Seeing my transformation
You made sure
That we never touched again

Allyson Moore

Aunts and Uncles

You cannot give me back
The innocence
Or the trust that I lost

You cannot give me the peace
The safety
Of a childhood that should have been nurturing

I am left with the shards
That still cut me
That send me into weeping times when memories
    surface again

You are as much to blame for this
As anyone
Accessories to sexual assault

COVER EXPOSURE

You stole my infancy
When I was raped by your drunken lovers
You stole my childhood
When you committed incest against me
You stole my teenaged years
By defiling my body
Seeking to control my intelligence
Suffocating my inner spirit

I want back what you took from me
You are a thief
No less a killer as well
It is time for your deeds
To be brought out forth from the dark
Where people can see them
Where the truth about you
Can be made known

MY BED

I love my bed
I take such delight in it
Soft pillows, pretty colors
Egyptian sheets
Delicate perfumed scents everywhere
A luxurious retreat for my tired body

At almost any time
I am eager to slip back between the covers
Where I feel warm
Held
Protected
Unlike emotions that I have ever felt towards a bed
before

Today I understood
Why I have never enjoyed sleep until now
While a bed is supposed to be a place
Of regeneration and love
It has always represented
A torture chamber for me

The Cow

It explains why I have always preferred
Sleeping somewhere else
For 59 years
I have never felt safe
In my own bed
Finally I do

Communion

All the other girls
Wore white patent leather shoes
You made me wear
Black

Having stripped me
Of my innocence
It now makes sense to me
Why I could not be the virgin bride

I stood out once again
Isolated by your actions
Freaked out
In my own misery

ANGRY TO DEATH

I sit on the examining table
Weeping in pain
Pushing back the tears
Attempting to hide my discomfort

My mother hated my body
In turn it is retaliating against me
Literally shedding off my own skin
Bloody looking masses of diseased flesh

My heart is no better
Ripped to shreds
It leaks
Worn out from the failure to be loved

My body absorbed her anger
Allowing it to settle into my joints
Which are now so damaged
I can barely walk nor play my beloved piano

Perhaps it is my body
Which is showing its anger now
Saying enough
That it is done

Allyson Moore

Bow on Your Knees

Get on your knees and pray
For your sinful soul
For the sins of Adam and Eve
For the transgressions of all who came before you

Get down you ignorant slut
Ask for forgiveness
With a contrite heart
Perhaps then I will stick fewer objects up your ass

Bow before me
Acknowledge that you are a sinner
Perhaps then God will be merciful
As that crazed look crossed her face again

GENDER DENIAL

I wanted a doll for Christmas
Someone whom I could love
And shower my attention upon

You gave me socks
Underwear
And a truck

Did you have to make it so obvious
That you wanted a boy
Instead of me?

Allyson Moore

WEDDING SUICIDE

The day that I came back from my honeymoon
On the island of St John
With Tim
You called

Naively
I thought that you had done so to welcome us back
To recount the beautiful moments of our wedding
To delight in our first activities as husband and wife

Heartlessly
You threatened to commit suicide
Head in the oven
Drowning yourself naked in the sea

A new bride come home to have her mother's blood
Splattered upon her
More jealous attempts
To destroy my happiness

CAPTIVITY

Shards of light
Shone through
The blackness of my existence

Giving me hope
Reminding me
Of the beauty that lay out there

Trapped in the prison
Of your abuse
I knew one day that I would be set free

Having been released
I have found that I can never fully escape
My captivity

WILL I EVER BE RID OF YOU?

Hopefully there will be a time
When it is done
When I will have released the pain
That still tortures me

If you were dead
I would begin to have some sort of closure
Knowing that you could not strike out at me
That I would not be subjected to your drunken
    phone calls

Yet I wonder
If I will ever truly be free of you
Worrying that I will always hold the capacity for you
    to wound me
Within

REFUGE?

Did I like closets?
Or did they represent another place where you hurt
   me?
I always thought that my need to be in them
Originated from me
To hide from you

Memories are beginning to surface
Traumas that I have suppressed
Scenes that I see
Putting into question the reality of what I thought
Were my childhood refuges

Were the family jokes and
My attempts to explain why I spent so much time in
   them
Indicative of another form of abuse
An excuse for it
Or a way of protecting my psyche?

The pattern will repeat itself
If there is any truth to it
Fragments of memories will gently surface
Until one day when I see the entire picture
And break down again

Confession

A long line always formed behind you
When you went to weekly confession
The time that you were on your knees
Detailing your sins to the priest
Seemed interminable

What could you have done in a week's time
That was so reprehensible?
I was unaware of any murdered bodies in the
     playroom
The maimed bodies of your daughters in their
     bedrooms
Likely did not count

Were there any penances issued
For the sins that you
Committed against your daughters?
Remorse, promises not to engage in those crimes
     again?
I think not

NO INTERCEPT

In the dawn
I woke up to the light
Saw that it was wondrous
Walked towards it

As I traversed the path
I came upon darkness
You were waiting to intercept me
I kept walking

You tore at my clothes
Stripped me of my self esteem
Defiled my body
But never infiltrated my soul

Allyson Moore

COUCHES

Odd though it may seem
I have an uncomfortable relationship with couches
Rarely have I ever been able to utilize
Them for any sort of socializing

While some of them have been quite lovely
With exquisite fabrics and innovative designs
I have never become attached to them
Never able to just sink into them and go ah . . . .

They have always fulfilled
Strictly utilitarian functions in my life
Places for the entertainment of my guests
Or as places to sleep to escape my own bed

Couches bring me back to the horrors of my
    childhood
Where my mother plied her clammy hands upon me
Touched me in inappropriate ways, encouraging me
    to touch her
My skin still crawls at the remembrance of it

THE CRIME

People say that we become like the gods
That we worship
Could it be that
We create the gods
That emulate
Who we are?

In the hands of some
Dogma attributed to a church
Is used as a weapon
To maim and to kill
The deception is in believing that this is god
When it is ourselves

Heinous
Unpunishable crimes
Are committed every day
Against those God's creations
The worst ones are perpetrated
Under the covers of darkness

CULPABLE

A mother's milk
Should have sustained life
No wonder
Yours were dry

You had nothing
To give
Of yourself
To others

Much less
To the children
That you chose
To bear

Your church did a terrible thing
In decreeing that it was sinful
To obstruct life
They are as culpable as you for the damage

INVISIBLE

I spent my childhood being invisible
Unheard
With no voice

When my husband
Did the same to me
I was devastated

I had assumed that everyone would listen to me
Once I began to speak
But this still wasn't true

I could not get my voice to be heard
It was over powered
Or dismissed

I live in a deaf world
Surrounded by people
Who do not hear me

Allyson Moore

FANTASY DESIGN

You tried to steal my femininity
Crushing it under the weight
Of your anger

You effectively removed any remnants that I was a girl
Short hair
Boyish clothes

Dark angular bedroom furniture
More suited for a man
Than a young woman

I wondered why you decorated
The rest of my room in a girlish manner
It was at such odds with how you dressed me

I now realize that you designed it for yourself
To enhance the fantasy
While you committed your sexual assaults upon me

DIABOLIC MIND

I was defenseless
Against a pervert
Masquerading as a mother

When I had grown up
I was capable of fighting you with words
But incapable of getting you to admit the truth

Your diabolic mind
Twisted everything that I said
Discounted every thought that I processed

The deeds were so horrifying
I had trouble believing them myself
Never getting you to own up to them

When at last the memories surfaced
There was no longer any doubt in my mind
That is when your rage went to another level

TRASHED

I am damaged goods
Battered
Broken
By your continuous assaults

You left your marks upon me
Making sure that once you were done with me
Any one else
Would be reviled

You entered my special sanctuary
Making sure that you destroyed it
That no one else
Would be able to enjoy the fruits that you had
     feasted upon

Your smug denial of your deeds
Further drove me into despair
While you enjoyed the perverse pleasure
Of knowing what you had gotten away with

NO ONE HEARS

There is no justice
For those who have suffered
Like I have
At the hands
Of their own mother

There is no redress in the courts
Childhood traumatic memories
Are negated as being fantasy
False reports
Vengeance against other wrongs

The family reacts in denial
They do not want to hear the accusations
Adding to the isolation
Worsening the pain
Protecting the perpetrator

I am anathema
For speaking the truth
Society discards me
Just as much as my family has
Following the precedent that my mother set

Allyson Moore

DRUNKEN STUPOR

One small space
I don't even know how I fit myself into it
Two sections of dressers joined together on one side

Into this narrow opening I squeezed myself
Hoping that I would be safe
Knowing that I would not be

I knew what was coming next
I would be dragged out by my hair or my feet
To be molested by my rage filled drunken mother

I was helpless to stop
The humiliations that were performed
Upon my body

My mind entered a place where I knew
The horrors that were being done to me
But where I could escape the shock

Once done she would silently abandon my battered
    body
Collapsing into a drunken stupor
To this day denying her actions

ENDURE

I entered a black soundless void
To escape the horrors
That were being done to me

Her touch sent me to a place of safety
To escape the brutality
Of this one

My head buried under the pillow
I believe that I went into shock
Some may call it the "other realms"

There were times when I saw
Gemstones and crystals shining brilliantly
Hidden in caverns that filled my fantasy world

Being young
I had endurance
Instinctively knowing that if I were compliant I
    would survive

To Live or to Experience

Some would say
You are my teacher
That without your abuse
I would have failed to explore
My inner depths like I have

I strongly disagree

It was suggested that because
I was brought up in affluence
That I needed to experience extreme loss
In order that I might be propelled
Down the path of self-discovery

Nonsense

Some people are born with compassion
That cannot be blighted
By the actions of a mentally ill person
It is a universal excuse
To justify not pursuing the perpetrator

FAÇADE

Before I understood
How full of hatred you were
I wanted to be like you

You had the tiniest waist
Slender hips
The most beautiful gowns

I would stand in your closet
Inhaling the perfumed fragrances
That clung to your garments

In awe of the delicate high heeled shoes
That you wore upon your feet
I dreamed of being elegant like you

When I realized that it was all a façade
I learned that while ugliness can be hidden
One day it will be exposed

Allyson Moore

SPANKING

She delighted in rolling down my panties
Ordering me to lie across her lap
Then calculatingly slapping my behind
With all her might

She liked to rub my buttocks slowly
As she blew that stink breath
Hot air across my cheeks
While I hung there helplessly

Whack!
Over and over again
The spankings were sexual
In every sense of the word

Many years later I understood
Why her face would flush
Her breathing become sharper
The look of satisfaction in her eyes

The Cow

Whether she held me as an older child
In this humiliation position
Or slapped me
As a prelude to inserting something inside me

The results were the same
These were perverse acts
Of sexual dominance
Against a minor

PARENT

Are you the parent?
Yes I am
How old are you?
19

Could you please come
To the high school guidance office?
Yes I will
I'll be there shortly

I no longer remember the details
Of that awful visit
I remember simply that my sister was in trouble
A parent was needed

That was me

I presented myself in my best mature persona
My goal being to save my sister
From whatever trouble
She had gotten herself into with the school

The Cow

Questions asked
I explained that I was providing a home for her
Absent father, abusive mother
A 19 year old caring for a 15 year old

I am 58 years old now
My own daughters are 19 and 15
Treacherous
Life defining ages

It is disturbing to me
That my parents abrogated their responsibilities
Leaving me to clean up their messes
To take over their roles

When I was still a young kid myself

Where is the justice in what happened?
There is none
They each hate me
I failed miserably

JUSTICE GOD

"God is not a god of love
He is a god of justice
Who metes out punishment
To the degree that it is earned"

How many times have I heard that in my life from
my mother?

"You are ignorant
Stupid
Naive
For believing that Jesus said that the greatest
commandment is to love"

"If you would only read the books
Of the theologians
Of the Catholic Church
You would know the truth"

I began proposing the idea during grammar school
That a person can have a one on one experience
with "God"
For that she branded me a heretic
That I was crazy; that I got it all wrong

It is easier to beat down your enemy
In this case me
Than to legitimately
Search for truth

Truth withstands all questions
That which is secret is not of the truth
That which bullies and intimidates
Does not come from love

Allyson Moore

GUILTY

I tried talking with you about this
Attempting to describe the memories
That were surfacing for me
Hoping that you would help make sense of them

Instead
You screamed at me
Calling me crazy
Shouting that I was bi-polar

Telling me that I should be locked up
To leave it alone
That I did not know what I was talking about
You were deflecting the truth

When I sought your help
I knew for sure that you were
Guilty
Of the desecration of my body

ALMOST HOMICIDE

Her anger was so extreme
That she did not want children
His anger was so extreme
That she did not want children
That he shot at her

The bullet narrowly missed her
Missing my sister whom she held
As it passed through the wall
Into my bedroom
Narrowly missing me

Who was he trying to kill?
Was he imitating the man in Smithfield
Who saw no other way to escape
His captivity
Than to murder his entire family?

Who was the worst potential murderer of the two?
The one who did not love and abandoned us
Or the one whose violent rages
And games with pistols and rifles
Sent clear messages about our possible fates?

HATRED

Where the rage came from
I do not know
I can only guess
Based upon the reading
That I have done throughout the years

I imagine that my mother hates herself
So badly
That she has to strike out at everything around her
Most especially
Her own issue

It is not hatred
Of me
That propels her
But hatred of herself
Which she denies

ANDROGYNY

Your sexual abuse
Rendered me androgynous
Neither male
Nor female
Save for the obvious trappings

I had no desire to appeal
To either gender
Once I understood that the abuse had been real
Much preferring the safety
Of non-attachment

I envy my girlfriends
Who are enthralled
By their womanhood
I want to reclaim that part of my life
But am afraid that I will never be able to do so again

As I process the memories and those that will
      continue to surface
I see that I am now taking joy
In the little things
That makes me a woman
I am beginning to love myself

LIVING

I provoked her fury
By just being

My existence was a catalyst
For her implosions

Thus once released
She was able to move on to weaker victims

While I remained
Reduced to rubble

HEART

What mother fails to tell their child
That they were born with a heart defect?
You bitch

In over 50 years
Did you not think that it was important to mention it?
Of course not

There is only one person
Who exists in your world
You

I was a uterine sack
Delivered from you
Then discarded

The damage done to my heart and lungs
From the withholding of this information
Almost killed me

ULCERS

It has disturbed me all these years
That you could remember so little medically about me
You bore me
Then abandoned me
Trash kicked to the side

The stress of living with you
Gave me such severe burning in my throat
That I thought
My heart
Was on fire

When I told the doctor
You laughed and humiliated me
I was a 10 year old crippled by the pain
Of bleeding ulcers
From the stress of living with you

HELP ME

I have never felt completely safe
Nor have I found that I can trust anyone
Who tells me that they will take care of me
And then proves that they will actually do so

Parents are supposed to provide security
Mine did not
One pillaged
While the other turned a blind eye

I struggle to maintain control over my life
Vowing to never allow anyone else
To rip it away from me again
But always fearful that someone will

Now in the days
When my body is broken
From the years of extreme abuse
I find it hard to allow anyone to help me

Allyson Moore

THE HOST

I have often teased
That my mother
Was the Host
That bore me

A sort of alien
Whose womb
Was borrowed
For the birth

A cervix
That opened
Dropping me alone
Into the world

It would explain
Her cold
Reptilian skin
Lack of heart

Behind the sentiment
There is a bitter reality
The joke
Concealing my pain

I THE MAN

There were no frills in my life
Anything that would have appeared
To feminize me
You took away
Denied me

I wanted the white communion dress
With lace and flowers
You decreed that I wore
A severe style
Almost mannish

I cried wearing it
I looked ugly
Just as you wished me to be
You tried to make me into a boy
For reasons that I still struggle to understand

ESCAPE

I gazed upon the horizon
Longing to be somewhere else
To escape the torment
Of my existence here

Windswept hair
Lifted by the drafts encircling me
I was lost in my imagination
A self-created respite

I have come to love this place
But long to be
Done with this chaos
To be with a family that loves me

I decided to live a life of unconditional love
Not wishing to sink to their levels
Hoping that they would find the good in me
And love me

Unsuccessful
I am weary
Perhaps I am not up to the task
I wish to leave

IMMOLATE

There are things that people
Will never understand
Even though
They say that they do

They can never know
The horror
That I felt
When I was violated

The hands on me
The crazy look in her eyes
The sensation of her breath upon my skin
The helplessness of it all

I was the rack upon which
Self-hatred was played out against itself
My body was the pyre
Where my mother sought to immolate herself

Never Could

Impenetrable
I could not make you like me
I could not make you want me
I could not make you want to love me

Heartless
I could not feel any tenderness from you
I could not feel any nurturing from you
I could not feel any love emanating from you

Devoid
Of any motherly instinct
I tried to get you to love me
But could not

INCEST

It started with the ritual of the Rosary
She would make me get on my knees
To pray it in front of her
Invoking the protection of a Blessed Mother
Who could not stop the lunatic who was my mother

My mind went numb
At that stage
As did my limbs
I feared what would follow next
Was powerless to prevent it

The lamb brought to the sacrificial bed
Lights out
The door closed
Time passed
The door re-opened

I was turned on to my belly
My ass lifted
Pajamas removed
My underwear rolled down
Objects then inserted into me

Allyson Moore

Under the cover of darkness and blankets
My special places violated
I never saw her face
But I could feel her breath
Smell the liquor

I do not know how I survived it
It were as though
I went to another place
Where I did not feel the pain
Nor the degradation that was done to me

When she had finished
She departed as quietly as she had come
While my shattered psyche
Reeled with the terrors
That she inflicted upon me

INDEPENDENT BIRTH

You gave birth to me
But did not give me life
I gave birth
To myself

Wholly independent from you
From the cutting of the umbilical cord
I strode out into the world
Untethered
But determined

Not knowing what you had lost
You seemed confused by my actions
Longing for something
Which you could not give me
I moved forward

Wishing for the nurturing
Which you could not provide
Searching for the gift of love
Which you had not received yourself

YOU

I had a hard time
Figuring out who I was
Because you never allowed me
To be who I am

You sought to destroy my identity
By inflicting yours upon mine
Strangling the life out of me
Destroying my center point of reference

I spent my existence in a sort of limbo
Largely emotionless
Unattached to anything
Desiring nothing

When at last I began to emerge
I did not know how to cope
With the me who insisted on coming into life
My world thrown into chaos

Age Inflicted

Growing up
I believed that my mother went crazy
In her 30's
After her surgery
Once she had found god

I viewed it as an illness
That silently crept up on someone
Stealing them
Leaving the empty shell
Of their body behind

I was afraid to become 30
Convinced that I too would be afflicted
By the same disease
Which destroyed my mother
Shattered my family

I asked and I prayed
That should such a fate befall me
That my time here
Should gently end
Not wishing to inflict this upon others

Allyson Moore

MURDER UNDETECTED

Your father killed your mother
Beating her as he always had
She fell breaking her arm
When a blood clot formed
She died
Putting her out of her misery

He escaped a murderer's sentence
A wall of silence erected around a man
Who killed his wife
Tormented his children
Driving all of them
Into alcoholism or mental illness

You in turn attempted to kill me
But I was much stronger
Than you expected
Although you physically dominated me
You made the mistake of believing that
You controlled me

The Cow

While my inability to speak up for myself
Suggested weakness
You mistook the strength that I was gaining
You never succeeded in breaking me
I did not descend into the hell and abuse
That you carried forth into your generation

Stripped naked
You got away with your perversions
Until now
I am taking you out from under the covers
Where all can see who you truly are
Exposing you

Allyson Moore

TRUTH REVEALED

I always thought that it was me
I believed the lies
That you told me
Until I discovered the truth

Although I was very social
I had few friends
No one ever came
Over to the house

I blamed myself

You always led me to believe that it was me
In my innocence
I accepted your words
Until I started thinking for myself

Away from you
I had a lot of friends
When they met you
They left me

I thought that it was me

The Cow

Until the day that I called our family doctor
When I was an adult
Seeking to know why my mother
Thought that I was crazy

In a gentle voice he told me
That I had been a delightful child
Friendly like a puppy
Nothing wrong with me

He had warned my father
To get me away from her
That she was mentally ill
Was determined to harm me

It was then that I knew that it was NOT me

JEALOUS

I was a beautiful child
Who did not deserve
The horrors that you
Inflicted upon me

Golden hair
Freckles across the bridge
Of my face
I was a pixie

Full of life
Filled with joy
Loving all those around me
A being that you were not

You were jealous of me
Possessing titian red hair
A tiny waist
You still could not bear the sight of me

I knew it in how
You looked at me
I felt it in how
You touched me

Killing Set in Motion

It was bad enough that you killed my father
He never recovered from you
Then you attacked me
I too will always be damaged

The worst thing was watching what you did to my
    sister
Bridget was weaker than me
She turned to drugs and psychiatric settings
To recover from the damage that you had done

Unfortunately she became you
Her delicate soul lost
Unable to process the magnitude of the horrors
That you wreaked upon her little body

Though living today
She died a long time ago
Her spirit seemingly departed
The shell striking out in anger against everyone

Allyson Moore

It's My Life

I lived life
Through your eyes
Not my own

I abandoned my passions
Because you killed mine
In doing so I became lost

Now empty
My eyes opened
I see the barrenness

Stark reality
Devoid of substance
I wish to get myself back

LOST OPPORTUNITY

You should have saved me
You knew exactly what she was doing
You admitted it in the months before you died
As though this would exonerate your soul
A death bed confession
Yes
I forgive you

Why didn't you do something to help us?
You had the opportunity to save two little girls
From a monster who was committing incest against
    them
From a father who was absent
In denial
In an altered state
When indeed he was around

Yet you did not intervene
With horror
I now understand that you knew the truth
You knew the signs of that abuse
But chose not to get involved
You protected her and yourself
But killed us

Accursed

Why did you call me a whore
When all of the neighbors talked behind your back
Accusing you of this perfidy?
Your cruel deflections stabbed at my innocence

The accuser becomes the accused
The accurser the accursed
The tramp
The gossip of the neighborhood

LOVING MYSELF

It has taken me
All of my life to
Find my voice

You stole it from me

It has taken me
All of my life
To find myself

You killed my spirit

It has taken me
All of my life to
Believe in myself

You undermined my self-confidence

It has taken me
Until now
To love myself

These are my first steps

MADISON

When your husband deserted you
You turned around to me
Demanding that I support you
After I had done so for a time
Suffered through new levels
Of abuse from you
I left with only the clothes upon my back

What mother treats her child like this?

I was not allowed to take any of my
Personal possessions
I walked out without my dog
Without my poetry
Without my pictures or my books
Temporarily abandoning my sister
Into the hands of that mad woman

What society allows their young to be subjected to
    this?

The Cow

In the aftermath I discovered that I had begun to
    save myself
My efforts to do so for my baby sister were less
    successful
Although I had a home for her within days
My mother would not let her go
Her fury against me
Against herself
Now displaced upon the weakest member of the
    family

Will I ever forgive myself?

Allyson Moore

ALL EVIDENCE TO THE CONTRARY

The bomb shelter in our basement
Was indicative of the manner
In which our lives were structured
It was a bunker mentality that we lived under

A years worth of food supplies
Stashed in an inner room
The promise that our world
Was going to end imminently

There was no planning for the future
College was not even discussed
The world was going to end
I was going to be dead

It was a sick way to live
No child should be taught such hopelessness
In a country
Where such evidence exists to the contrary

My Sister

She does not love you
Her boyfriend, her job, her trips to the church
Are all more important than you

I picked you up
To bring you to my home
For the night

Knowing that you needed nurturing
A loving space
Away from her drama

Your eyes downcast
You wouldn't even look at me
I ached at seeing you be so withdrawn

When I asked you how you were
Your terse answer was
FINE

But I knew that you were not
A mother's love is the most important gift in the world
And she would not give it to you

Sacrificial Victim

If you hadn't pounded me as though it were your
    right to do so
I would have had more confidence
At times I am a child
In an adult body
Trying to act fearless
When I am not

If you had not criticized everything that I ever did
I would have trust in my abilities
Instead I continually second guess myself
Going endlessly in circles
Before I have the capacity
To act as the authority that I am

If you had lived the truths of the lies that you told
You would not have destroyed me
Forcing me to bend to your deranged will
It is my responsibility to climb out of the pit
That you threw me in
A martyr for your lifelong drama

MENSES

She dressed in a long sexy negligee
A shimmery
Diaphanous
Covering over it
Loosely bound at the waist
It accented her breasts
Which were protruding

Draping herself artistically on the settee
Wine glass in hand
She called me to join her
I was nervous
Not knowing what to expect
Yet fearing it
I sat as far away from her as I was able

"Come sit here Little Allyson"
"With MOTHER"
She shrieked in that commanding
Slurring
Sing song sort of voice
Which she employed when she was drunk
Scaring me

Allyson Moore

Reluctant though I was
Having already protested
She patted the spot directly in front of her
Insisting that I sat there
As her body wrapped itself around me
Her alcohol induced breath
Nauseating me

She turned to refill her glass from the decanter
Next to her
As she did
Her erect nipple
Popped out of her gown
Dragging across my face
I silenced the screams inside of me

After a long gulp
In which she finished its contents
She lowered her jaw to her chest
As she began to babble
Almost incoherently about the mysteries
Of becoming a woman
None of it relevant to the facts at hand

The Cow

There was no escape
From the agony of that ordeal
No safe place within my home
The memories as fresh as though they happened
    yesterday
I am still repulsed
By those enormous fat nipples that continually
Pressed into my face

When she passed out
I escaped the torture
Though I am still scarred by it

Allyson Moore

MOTHER MARY

Mother Mary
Why did you abandon me?
Why did you allow her to do those things to me?
Why didn't you stop her?

Mother Mary
I am your child too
You were supposed to protect me against all evil
To be my surrogate mother

Why was I alone?
Why weren't you there in the blackness?
Holding me?
Loving me?

Where were you Mother Mary?
Were you only there for her
Because she cried out your name during each act
That she performed against me?

BLOW

She raised her arm
To hit me in the face
With a hairbrush

I crossed my hands
In front of it
To deflect the blow

But fell sideways
As the bristles
Tore at my open lips

Although I was almost as tall
As she was
I was unable to defend myself

I no longer remember
What I had done
To send her into this fury

It didn't matter
She was releasing
Her own inner anger upon me

Eyes glazed over
My mother didn't
Even see me

It was rage
And alcohol
That fueled her

Murderer

You laughed at every one
Of my accomplishments
When I was growing up
I took them to heart
Thus abandoning my passions
Never developing ambition
Nor confidence in myself

When I began to show an aptitude
For drawing
You ridiculed me in front of Uncle Patrick
Stating that I never completed anything
Then pointing out how amateur
My attempts were
I never drew again

When I began to show my love for the piano
You made arrangements for me
To be given my great-grandmothers upright
Then shrieked loudly
When my ear twitched every time I hit an incorrect
    note
Insulting me in front of my grandfather
In turn you killed that passion as well

When I began to write poetry
Creating scrapbooks for the words I wrote
Set against my own photography
You said that they were childish
Empty
Lacking in sophistication
I did not write again for more than thirty years

Some women eat their young
By slowly torturing them
Murdering their spirits
Squeezing the life out of them
This is nothing less
Than you did to me
Mother

Nietzsche and Kierkegaard

Nietzsche and Kierkegaard
Have become my friends
In spite of your best efforts
To suppress me
From reading them

Screaming at me
You often called me
DANGEROUS
It was my mind that you told me
That you feared

The "God Questions"
Were my most passionate pursuits
I sought to understand
The universe and myself
You were afraid of the answers that I would receive

Eventually I found these friends
Wandering the maze of my own mind
I encountered them at the base
Of the tree of knowledge
That had been planted

Allyson Moore

No One Wants the Responsibility

How does a person ever get over it?
How can they even acknowledge to themselves
Or to the world
The atrocities that were done
But not seen by others?

There is no validation
Unless others recognize the abuse
Are willing to condemn it
It is safer to be in denial
Than to pretend that it exists

Mothers are not supposed to molest their daughters
Sticking foreign objects up their anus'
Violating their holy temples
It should be against the laws of nature
But sadly, is not

PENALTY BOX

Her cruelty became more extreme
The longer she got away with the incest
Her behavior more bizarre
As she escaped detection

Liquor gave her the semblance
Of additional authority
As she further lost any traces of morality
Or contact with reality

The confessional became a weekly sort of penalty box
Where she could confess her sins
Then climb back into bed again
To repeat them

Princess

You loved our dog Princess
More than you loved me
Thirty-five years after her death
You still weep
Your wailing a sickening display of inappropriate
    emotion

She had little attachment to you
Your drunkenness confused her
Awkward handling on your part
Causing her to look to me
For reassurance

Your false bereavement
Is an abomination
A divisive act
A sickening reminder
That you wanted her and not me

SELF CENTERED DRINKING

I stood at the queue for departing
School buses
Hair soaking wet from the rain
Clothes drenched
Miserable

I had called to say good bye
Before I left for the overnight
At Donna's
To celebrate her birthday
A rite of passage for young girls

Barely coherent
You screamed at me
Demanding that I come home instead
Drunk with Aunt Moira at 2 in the afternoon
Nastier than usual

Devastated I stood there
Embarrassed as I shared
How cruel you were with my friends
Knowing what I faced when I got home
Hurt that you could be so mean to me

Consoling me with hugs
They piled into the car
The bonding of sisters
While you isolated me again
A pillar of loneliness

PLEADING THE FIFTH

I saw you sneaking a long chug
Out of that bottle of Four Roses Whiskey
As I turned the corner into the kitchen
You spluttered in shock
At being caught with your dirty secret

Drinking from the concealed gallon
Hidden behind the potato chips
In the cabinet above the refrigerator
You had to stand on your tippy toes to reach it
If you hadn't been so angry it would have been funny

You screamed at me
Slapping me across the face
Startled
I froze
Unable to move

As I slowly regained my wits
My legs acted for me
Propelling me out of the room
I was too young to understand what it meant in that
        moment
In later years thankful for having witnessed her
        secret

Allyson Moore

NO ONE ESCAPES

Life should have flowed from your body
All of us were created with the same ability
Death however flowed through your veins
You sought to kill

Unable
Unwilling
To do it to yourself
You did so to those around you

No one escaped from you
No one knew how to control you
Today
People are still afraid of you

Your demonic fury
Your far reaching threats
To instill physical and legal harm
Silenced any who would stand up to you

MY MIND ABANDONED ME

I was abandoned by my mother
Whose self absorption was so extreme
That she viewed me
As an impediment to her happiness
My birth a pox
Forced upon her by societal standards

I was abandoned by my father
Whose self absorption was so extreme
That he focused on his career
Mired in his own mental illness
The test pilot escaped into the heavens
Where he could not hear my pleas for help

I was abandoned by my extended family
Whose self absorption and fear were so extreme
That they distanced themselves far away from my
    parents
And in turn, me
To escape the maelstrom
Lest they be get caught up in it

Allyson Moore

In the end it was my mind that abandoned me
Perhaps it was keeping me safe
From the memories of the trauma
Emotional scars being insufficient proof for a court
When I saw what had been done to me
The floodgates opened and the bleeding began again

PROFESSIONAL MOTHER

Her title was
Mother
Not Mama
Mom
Mommy
It was Mother

Called by any other name
She became stern
"My name is Mother"
In those steely words
I felt no love
Just a professional doing her job

It was obvious that she resented motherhood
Blaming me for foisting it upon her
Rather than simply keeping her legs shut
Or risking eternal damnation by using birth control
In not doing so
She condemned us both

Allyson Moore

BECOMING REAL

I never understood what the dreams meant
There would be fragments
Of events that I did not understand

Mostly I felt like I stood outside myself
Observing heinous things
That were being done to me

I felt detached
Disconnected from the images that I saw
Having the safety of sleep to protect me

I suppose that when my body was ready
The pieces began to come together
It was then that I understood that they were real

Sudden Recognition

The screams that I heard were my own
I looked quickly around the office
To see if anyone else had noticed my panic
Thankfully no one had

I was in my mid 40's
Managing portfolios worth millions
When I suddenly "heard" my sister screaming
"Saw" myself hiding for protection

Knowing that I was next
I collapsed in my office
Sobbing
Finally comprehending what had haunted me for
    years

Repulsed

I am repulsed by your touch
Every time you come near me
My skin crawls
My body instinctively recoils

Constantly trying to invade my space
You step forward
I step back
The social cues ignored

Leaning forward
Your big cow breasts
Are forever straining
To be in my face

It is loathsome to me
I want to run somewhere
To vomit
You out of me

LACK OF COMMUNICATION

My parents communicated with each other thru
Notes that were tied to a string
Hanging from the overhead light
In the kitchen

My mother didn't even try that hard to talk with me
I desperately wanted her to love me
To show an interest in me
But she was incapable of doing so

As I attempted to build a relationship with her
She laughed at me accusing me of being arrogant
Having no respect for herself
There was none left over for me

Allyson Moore

FINGERED

How could the hands
That fingered rosary beads
Be the same ones
That fingered me

The sanctity of the one
Is destroyed
By the depravity
Of the other

SCARS

There is no safety
For the tortured
Abused soul

One must abandon
The body
To seek the relief

Yet the body
Is not abandoned so quickly
Scars always remain

Allyson Moore

SHAM

Pocketbook in hand
The perfect hat
Poised on the perfectly coiffed hair
We slowly made our way into Mass
Putting on the show that she wanted everyone to see

Flanked by younger versions of herself
Albeit in dresses that lacked the New York
    sophistication of hers
The Italians in our parish snickered behind our backs
About the "lace curtain Irish"
And the uppity nouveau riche

Sadly there was nothing behind the windows
Nothing behind the show
It was all a sham
After being told that we were sinful creatures
We would be brought home to be ignored

ALERT TO ATTACK

Some women eat their young
Once they have gotten the taste
For that blood
They cannot stop

Such is the case with my mother
Who in her 80's
Thinks that taunting me
Is a blood sport

It would be logical to think
That I had learned
How to emotionally protect myself
But this is not always the case

She still strikes out
Wounds me in new ways
Is able to reach into my core
Turning me into that frightened child again

SISTER

Allyson Moore

She blames me for what happened to her
I blame myself
As the older sister I was supposed to protect her
From the evil that called itself
Our mother

I think that she hates me for not stopping
The physical and sexual abuse
That was inflicted upon her
For those reasons I think
That I have hated myself as well

I love her although I think that she hates me
What was done to her
Was done to me also
She must have heard my screams too
And not been able to do anything about it either

The Cow

The reasons why we have not had a relationship
In more than 30 years are complicated
By the impact of the abuses and how we dealt with
    them
While I ran headlong into marriages
She escaped into drugs and psychiatric settings

My baby sister was a beautiful child
Neither of us deserves what was done to us
The fact that neither of us will allow their children
Near their grandmother
Says everything

REPTILIAN

Allyson Moore

Reptiles move stealthily across the plain
Averting detection from their victims
Sudden precise attacks
Immobilize their prey

You are that snake slithering under the covers
Avoiding exposure
Striking at the throat
Swallowing your victims

Your scaling skin with
Round brown patches of pigment
Give you the appearance
Of man's most hated animal

It is ironic that your form
Has followed its function
Society not yet seeing you
For the danger that you are

STANDING UP

Evil should be stopped
You are the devil incarnate
No matter which hell
You climbed out of
Whether it is in your mind
Emanates from a creed of your church
Or you are possessed by an entity
You need to be stopped

Everyone is afraid of you
Your lawsuits
Threats of financial ruin
Theft of family monies
Have made it impossible
For any one to fight you
That is why you hate me
I have always stood up to you

Allyson Moore

WEEPING MARY

The weeping statue stood in the corner of the parlor
Figuratively
Spilling tears for the sins of mankind

While its caretaker
Stood by its side
Noticing the silent tears of the daughters

She invited us into the solarium to sit with her
After an uncomfortable silence
She extended her friendship

Peggy took the risk of stating
That she understood what was transpiring in our
    household
She wanted to help

I stared back at her
Trying to determine if she could be trusted
Afraid to be caught in an act of family treason

The Cow

She said that our Mother kept us in a closet
Dressing us up and trotting us out for these
    occasions of show
Then locking us up again

Dumbfounded she gave us her phone number
In case we ever needed her
In those moments she gave me hope

PARANOIA

Allyson Moore

Her paranoia was extreme
There was always a conspiracy
Behind every event
A person
Organization
Or thing
Out to get her

At the height of it
Her eyes would dart back and forth
Quickly
A manic quality to her actions
Heavy breathing
Loud
Staccato speech

There was no reasoning with her
She was mad
Literally
Beyond a child's reach
To help her
Locked within her own private hell
Lashing out at all those around her

The Cow

When the storm would quiet
She would pass out
Suspended in an alcoholic stupor
Or gleeful
That she had inflicted pain
Upon a victim
Who could not speak for themselves

SURROGATE MOM

Allyson Moore

I sought a mother figure
In each mature woman
Who showed any interest in me

I was desperate
To the point of embarrassment
For that sort of caring

Those who shared their love
With me the most
Died early

Sister Anastasia
Aunt Millicent
Barbara

I was bereft
My heart torn out
With each one of their passings

I clung to the pieces of themselves
That they had instilled in me
Grateful for their love

Yet I was still alone
My neediness for a surrogate mom
abated

Do Not Talk with Them

"Do not speak with an adult as though you are her
    equal"
As my mother yelled these words at me
She smacked me in the head
In front of her circle of friends
Dragging me onto the driveway
Where she gave me even worse hell

That violent explosion
Served its purpose
I never went near her friends again
Simply being too embarrassed to do so
No longer able to look any of them in the eye
I was the shamed dog with its tail between its legs

My mother succeeded in isolating me even further
It had not been arrogance on my part as she had
    claimed
That had made me wish to engage in conversation
    with them
It was the longing for anyone who could talk beyond
    kid babble
Who recognized me as a person
Who would talk with me

THE BEATING

Allyson Moore

She raised her arm to hit me
With the bristle brush
I knew that she intended to hurt me
Her eyes were glazed over and vacant

It were as though someone else possessed her body
She was going to inflict her pain upon me
Until she thought that I was remorseful enough
For whatever transgression she felt justified her
    actions

I put my arms up in front of my face to protect
    myself
Knowing that her first blow was always there
Perhaps if she took away my face
She would stop seeing hers

My hands deflected the charge somewhat
Bristles tearing at my lips only
As I stumbled sideways
Losing my balance

The Cow

In her rage ungodly sounds poured out of her
With the second blow
The brush achieved full impact with my face
It's hard wooden handle striking my jaw for extra
    measure

Beaten like an animal
I was defenseless
As she backed me into a corner
Of the basement

My mind screaming at the injustice of this
I wanted her to stop
But knew that she wouldn't
She had crossed into another realm

I smelled the reason
Whiskey
I heard her reason
God

Raging out of control
I knew where the third blow would land
I braced against the wall
As she struck me in my breasts

NOTHING MORE TO EXPECT

Allyson Moore

Big fat cow tongue
Sways back and forth
As she lowers her head to eat the grasses

Her eyes dull and lifeless
She does not care about the calf
At her side

She seems to be annoyed at its actions
The baby wants to play
She wants no part of it

As her hind leg lifts
She kicks it aside
Then proceeds to relieve herself

THE REMAINS

I watched you abuse my father
When he left you
You moved on to me

I became your next target
When I left you
You moved on to my sister

As each of us left
You turned your sights upon
The remaining victims

You tore the skin off our bodies
Tried to pluck the lives out of us
Dismembered us

Not seeing our carcasses
You still picked at the bones
Never abandoning your vulture like habits

SIGNS OF TROUBLE

Allyson Moore

How much more liquor will it take
Until your pain hits its peak?
It is then that I know
That you will begin
To inflict it upon me

I watch for the signs
Your hands begin to tremble
The corners of your eyes begin to droop
As they begin to get glassy
Then moist

Mostly it is the dramatic tone of your voice
That warns me
Slurring speech
Gives way to high pitched screeching
Accompanied by grandiose hand gestures

When I think that the attack is about to begin
I run down the hallway
Attempt to find a hiding place
Knowing that I will resist
Succumbing to the inevitable

VATICAN DECEPTION

We were my mother's window dressing at the Vatican
The old princes of the Church
Delighting in the fresh air that little girls
Brought in with them

They seemed to want to pay more attention to us
Than to the strident manner
In which my mother
Presented her documentation against sex education

It was easy to see
That she was oblivious to their lack of interest
They disdained Americans
Unless they came carrying the scent of money

It was a game that I later learned that they enjoyed
They grinned at me
I smiled back
The truth was understood

Allyson Moore

THE WHORE OF HALLOWEEN

I am the whore of Time's Square
That is what my mother believed
One Halloween night when she was drunk
Freaking out
That I had the kids out
Trick or treating
Until 9:30 pm

I was so disturbed
By her irrationality
Her lack of faith in my parenting
That I mischievously teased
That I had spent the evening hooking in New York
My mother thought so little of me that
She believed this to be true

She screeched in response
Became apoplectic
Stuttering
Literally spitting through the phone
Unable to discern reality for herself
In her drunken stupor
Inflicting her sick hell upon me

The Cow

She demanded to know where her children were
Yes
Her children
From their birth
They were not mine
They were hers
I was irrelevant

The whore that night was not me
Descending into madness
On the night when the veils between the worlds are
    thin
When the feel of death surrounds us
She sold her soul to the dark side
Her body
To the whiskey bottle

Allyson Moore

To All the Addison's

The pain of her mothers dismissal
Etched upon her face
Brought pain to mine
As I lived Addison's struggles

It is only a TV show
But the pathos created
Was a reflection of the relationship
That I have with my own mother

The self-centered seeking
Of her own happiness
At the expense of her daughter's
Was a cold reminder of my own reality

A part of me wanted to reach out to hug Addison
Knowing that she will never measure up
To her mothers cruelty
Hoping that we both heal

TODDLER RAPE

As she lay drunk on the sofa
In the living room of the apartment
That we resided in
He entered my room

Despite the fact that I slept in a crib
I can still see him
I was afraid of him
I had every right to be

My mother was going to do nothing to protect me
In fact it was her drunken affair
While my father was traveling
That resulted in this horrible man hurting me

I can see myself
Backing into the furthest point of my cage
As though I had crossed the room to observe
What was going to transpire

He was a cruel man
Who laughed as he hit me
Penetrated me
Then returned for more at another time

Allyson Moore

TRANSPARENCY

You took advantage of me
Because I was completely transparent
Born as it were without skin
Without protection
From the beast that sought
To devour me

You are the terror of the night
Stalking your prey
The lowly scum sent
To defile your daughter
Seeking to make her into your own image
Failing wretchedly

My inner light intact
You could not shatter the glass
My higher purpose known
The love I hold inside
Overwhelmed you
Drove you back into the darkness

NAÏVE TWIT

At 19 years of age
I was rescuing my under-age sister from dive bars
While my mother sat comatose
Every night drunk and inert

I did so without question
Without judgment
Believing that family stuck together
Protected each other

I was a naïve twit
Perhaps I prevented her from being raped
But in the end
She hated me nonetheless

Allyson Moore

THE TYRANT

Your Catholic religion
Was not your god
You were its figurehead
Appointing yourself the ruler
Determining your own form of justice
Subjugating your slaves
To your demands

Offering no compassion
No love
In your deeds
You are a tyrant
Delighting in hurting your children
Your actions a measure
Of your own self hatred

MEMORIES

I had the oddest
Most unexpected experiences
Regarding my emotions
When I was pregnant with my eldest

For reasons that I did not understand
Until later
I was worried that if she were born a girl
That I would molest her

I was filled with fear
Not understanding
Recoiling interiorly
From the implications of those thoughts

I would rather have been dead
Than to do those things to my child
It was with relief when she was born
That I was not afflicted by those perversions

Allyson Moore

Violation

Powerless
I lay there
As though bound
Yet no ropes were attached

Helpless
I could only close my eyes
Sliding into an unknown world
Until it was over

I could not defend myself
I'm not sure that I even understood
What was happening to me
Relieved when it was over

I was violated
The smell of her and her liquor
Remained on my body
The emotional bruises taking longer to heal

INWARD/OUTWARD

They pitied me
The girls
The nuns
Even the staff

Every one in my high school
Knew how crazy you were
So they felt sorry for me
But largely I was left alone

No one wants to engage
In others troubles
They might rub off
Become their problems

I turned inward
Found light and contentment within
The outward
Was just too horrifying to deal with

Allyson Moore

WOODS

Craving sanctuary
I instinctively
Headed to the woods
Where I could blend in
Not be seen

I sought the darkened hues
Where no one would notice me
No one would seek me out
I could be hidden
And thus survive

What trauma was this
That I was driven to those depths?
A trauma so severe
That I nearly lost my life
Saved by the nature that nurtured my battered spirit

CHOICE

If you didn't want me
Why didn't you give me to someone who would?
You would have spared us both the misery
Of being stuck with each other

In a perverse way
I do think that you wanted me
As a sadistic recipient
For your own self hatred

To have given me up
Would have been an act of unselfishness
Something of which
You are not capable

Allyson's Requiem

Before us lies the body of
Allyson Moore
Battered
Broken

She could not withstand the onslaught
Of a lifetime of hatred and abuse
That was heaped
Upon her by her Mother

In life
This child of light
Shone like a candle
Sending love to all who came in contact with her

Keeping the wounds hidden
She sought to transform her Mother's
Viciousness
Into love

In the end
She lost the battle
Her heart repeatedly shattered
By her Mother's unwillingness to love her

THE COW

Although I have sought peace
I have not yet found it
Having to settle instead
For contentment

Joyous childhoods
Should lead
To fulfilling
Adulthoods

Having determined at a young age
That my mother
Was no more than a cow
My expectations were lowered

She had made it clear
That she had not wanted me
But that a mother's instinct kicked in
When she first saw me

Allyson Moore

Huge hanging teats
She were as though a farm animal
With her big nipples forever exposed
Pressing into my face

Cows stand in pastures
Shitting where they stand
Giving birth
Then abandoning their calves for slaughter

LOCKING THE GATE

Cows are supposed to live in pastures
Or zoos
Not be allowed free
To roam into peoples lives
Dropping
Cow patties
Wherever they go

Sad to say
My mother's instincts
Never kicked in
She more or less
Stomped on me
Whenever she moved
To another part of the field

It is time
To lock her out
So she can find
Another herd

A Final Note

In the days before she died when she babbled nonsensically, my mother looked me in the eyes for one clear moment and stated that she was sorry for everything that she had done to me. I told her that I loved her as she slipped into oblivion.